INSPIRATIONAL
SHORT STORI
YOUNG READERS
CW00455534
2:0

The trademarks that are used are without any consent, and the publication of the trademark is without permission or backing by the trademark owner. All trademarks and brands within this book are for clarifying purposes only and are the owned by the owners themselves, not affiliated with this document.

Table of Contents

INTRODUCTION: THE MAGIC OF SOCCER

If you're holding this book, you're probably already a soccer fan, or maybe you're just interested in why so many people love this sport. Whether you're an experienced player, a fan of watching games, or just someone who loves a good story, you're about to go on an exciting trip. These stories are all about the magic of working as a team, the players' unwavering commitment, and the amazing things that can happen when we all speak the same language of soccer.

Soccer, which is often called "the beautiful game," is played all over the world. It's more than just a sport; it's a hobby that brings people from all walks of life together. Kids can play soccer on the biggest stages in the biggest stadiums, on dusty fields in the smallest towns, and even in their own backyards. No matter where you are in the world, soccer is there. The simple joy of chasing a ball and working as a team to score goals brings people and towns together.

As you read this book, you'll come across amazing stories that show how soccer can inspire and bring people together. From the busy streets of India to the snowy fields of the Nordic countries, from the rocky terrains of Afghanistan to the heartwarming moments of unity on international grounds, these stories will show you that soccer is more than just a game—it's a source of hope, friendship, and the kind of magic that can bring people together in amazing ways. So, young explorers, let's start our trip

into the magical world of soccer and find the stories that will warm your heart and give you hope.

Thanks again for choosing this book, make sure to leave a short review on Amazon if you enjoy it. I'd really love to hear your thoughts

CHAPTER 1: MARIA'S EARLY GOALS

There was a sunny town called Dois Riachos in the middle of Brazil. The palm trees slowly swayed, and children's laughter could be heard in the streets. One of the kids there was a little girl with a big, bright smile. She was called Maria.

Maria played football in a way that no one else did. Instead of buying a shiny ball, she had old socks tightly wound together to make one. Many people might have thought it was strange or even funny. But that sock-ball meant a lot to Maria. She was always with her and went on many trips with her through the winding streets of Dois Riachos.

While other kids chased butterflies or played hide-and-seek, Maria could be found dribbling her favorite ball, practicing shots, and dreaming of big venues. Some people might not have thought it was real football, but Maria saw it as the key to her dreams.

<u>Doubters and Dreamers</u>

When the school bell rang at the end of the day, Maria would run home, do her chores, and then head right to the dusty streets of Dois Riachos. There, she would play her heart out as the orange and pink colors of the setting sun painted the sky. She dribbled the ball around trees as if they were players from the other team and shot at goals that didn't exist.

But not everyone could understand Maria's drive. She was often followed by giggles and whispers. Some kids would say, "Girls don't play football!" with a teasing smile. But Maria never let doubts get in the way of her dreams. She had fire in her eyes and a strong will. She would answer confidently, with her hands on her hips, "I'll play for Brazil one day, just you wait and see!" Even though some kids laughed at her bold claim, her family stood around her like a wall to protect her. They knew she had great promise, so they would always tell her, "Dream big, Maria!"

The City Coach's Visit

In the small town of Dois Riachos, where everyone knew each other, news spread quickly. And when people heard how good Maria was at soccer, the word spread like wildfire. Stories about the little girl with unbeatable skills and her sock-ball spread beyond her town and into the busy streets of Brazil's bigger cities.

On a sunny day, a coach who was good at spotting potential went to Dois Riachos. He had heard about Maria and wanted to see for himself what all the fuss was about. As he watched her play, he couldn't believe how she was able to get around other players and make amazing goals. He could see how talented Maria was and how much she could grow. As he walked up to her, he told her, "You have a gift, young lady." Then he gave her a chance she had only ever dreamed of: she could train in the big city with top-notch teachers and facilities. Even though it was a golden ticket, she had to leave her family and the place she loved so much.

Maria was confused. She was drawn to the city lights, but leaving home made her heart feel heavy. But her family, who had always been her rock, came forward. They had faith in her and her

dreams. With their support and the promise that they would always be there for her, Maria found the courage to follow her dream and take her first big step toward becoming a famous football player.

Big City, Bigger Dreams

Maria felt like she was in a different world in the city, with its tall buildings, constant noise of cars, and huge football grounds. Everywhere she looked, people who had been training for years were showing off skills she had never seen before. The fields were no longer dirty like they were in Dois Riachos. Instead, they were huge, green fields that seemed to go on forever.

But whenever Maria felt stressed or out of place, she would close her eyes and think back to how she had started out. She would think about the dirty streets, the shade of the palm trees, and her favorite sock-ball. Those memories made her think about what she was passionate about and the trip she had taken. Maria's determination only got stronger as she thought about these memories. She was determined to give it her all, no matter how hard the training sessions got or how skilled her friends seemed.

Maria was always there, rain or shine. She was the first one there and the last one to leave the exercise ground. She worked hard at it every day, learning, changing, and getting better. She knew in her heart that this place was just another part of her story, and she was ready to make the most of it.

Wearing the Colors of Brazil

In Dois Riachos, people talked and did exciting things every day. Maria, who was the pride of the small town, had done something great. No one had missed her countless hours of practice, her unwavering energy, or her skills that couldn't be beat. The news that Maria had been chosen to wear the famous yellow and green shirt of Brazil made the whole town excited.

Every time she played a match, she carried the hopes and dreams of the many people who had watched her grow up. Every time she stepped onto one of the huge football fields, it wasn't just a game; it was a performance full of emotion and hard work. She ran, dribbled, and tackled while promoting herself, her country, and her hometown.

When she touched the ball in Dois Riachos, people would cheer in the streets. Everyone was happy and proud of every goal she scored and every move she made. Maria was no longer just a little girl with big dreams. She had become a source of hope and motivation, showing everyone that dreams, no matter how big, can come true.

A Hometown Hero

In the small streets of Dois Riachos, a change was happening. Once quiet, the streets were now filled with the laughing of kids playing football, and Maria's name was always at the center of their games. They had heard stories about her from their parents and seen how fascinating her games were on old TVs. Maria wasn't just a soccer player to them; she was a hero from their own land.

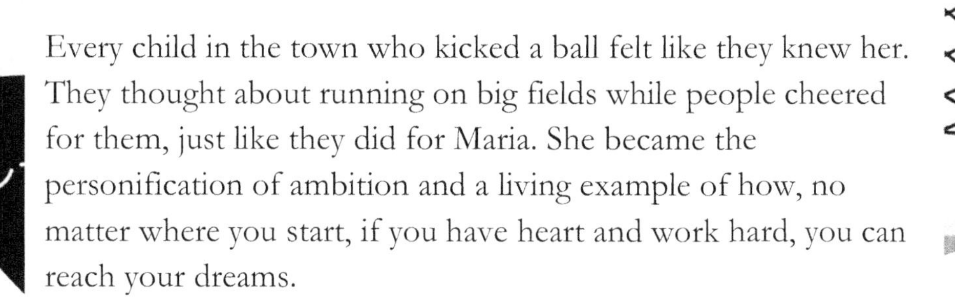

Every child in the town who kicked a ball felt like they knew her. They thought about running on big fields while people cheered for them, just like they did for Maria. She became the personification of ambition and a living example of how, no matter where you start, if you have heart and work hard, you can reach your dreams.

When people got together in Dois Riachos, they often talked about Maria's adventures. Every story about her, from her first goal on the world stage to her amazing saves, was a source of inspiration. Through Maria, the kids in the town learned an important lesson: where they came from didn't determine their future; their dreams did.

Dream Big, Play Joyfully

Maria's path to stardom was paved with more than just trophies and accolades. At the heart of her journey was an unwavering love for football. Every time she set foot on the pitch, it was evident in her eyes, her moves, her spirit. Winning mattered, but what mattered more was the sheer joy of playing, the magic of being one with the ball.

This was the essence of Maria's story. It wasn't merely about the heights she reached but the passion that propelled her there. Through rain or sunshine, in victories or defeats, her dedication remained constant. Her story whispered to the world a simple truth: dreams fueled by genuine love and hard work have the power to transcend any boundary.

And so, in the annals of football history, Maria stood out not just as a player of great skill but as a beacon of inspiration. Her journey echoed a timeless lesson: to achieve greatness, one must dream grandly and play with an unbridled sense of joy.

This inspiring story takes cues from the remarkable journey of Marta Vieira da Silva, a soccer legend whose determination and passion led her from a small town in Brazil to soccer greatness.

CHAPTER 2: LEO'S GROWTH CHALLENGE

Rosario, a busy city, was right in the middle of Argentina. A young boy named Leo stood out among the busy streets and bright buildings. A simple leather ball was the center of his world. With every touch, kick, and run, it was clear that Leo and soccer went together like nothing else.

Leo would go to the neighborhood soccer field every night as the sun was turning the sky orange and gold. It wasn't the best place in the world, but to Leo, it was a place where anything could happen. As the cool breeze of Rosario blew by, he would do magic with his feet, dribbling past opponents that didn't exist, throwing to teammates that didn't exist, and scoring amazing goals. In his lively mind, the rusty goalposts and patchy grass under his feet turned into the best stadiums in the world.

For those who got to see it, it was a beautiful sight. Leo wasn't just playing; he was putting on a show, expressing himself, and thinking. Every day, Leo's heart and feet danced in time to the city's famous sunset, painting stories of big dreams and even bigger hopes, all centered around the beautiful game of soccer.

<u>Whispers of a Challenge</u>

As time went on, there was a clear change. Many of Leo's friends started to grow, and as each month went by, their shapes got bigger. Then Leo? He didn't change much, and his small size became more noticeable as his friends got taller.

Leo's folks, who are always helpful and aware, also noticed this. With worry written all over their faces, they went to see doctors. After a few trips and tests, they found out that Leo had a lack of growth hormone. Because of this, Leo might never grow up to be as tall as his friends and teachers. The truth hit them hard and made their hearts feel heavy. They knew that getting to play professional football would be hard, and they knew that physical problems could be an extra struggle.

Rosario slowly found out what was wrong with Leo. People were whispering, and many of them wondered if Leo's hopes of becoming a football star were too big. Some talked about their worries out loud, while others just gave each other knowing looks. In the middle of the whispers and quiet doubts, there was one burning question: Could the boy who loved the game more than anyone else handle this unexpected challenge?

An Unexpected Opportunity

Talent speaks for itself, and it can be heard far beyond the limits of a city and across huge oceans. So many people talked about how good Leo was with the ball. Even though Rosario still had doubts, stories of a young boy with amazing skills started to spread across countries. Soon, scouts from a well-known football club in Europe heard these stories, which talked about how good Leo was at moving and how he seemed to see everything on the field.

The club was interested right away because it had a lot of money and was known all over the world. They looked past the numbers and figures that other clubs might be obsessed with. Instead, they

saw that Leo had raw ability that couldn't be denied. They not only saw a future sports star in him, but they also felt like it was their duty to help him develop his talent. In an act of kindness, they offered to pay for his medical care and asked him to join their prestigious youth academy.

The offer was both exciting and scary for Leo and his family. On the one hand, it was a chance for Leo to learn at one of the best academies in the world, a golden ticket that would help him improve his skills and get closer to his goals. On the other hand, it meant stepping into the unknown and leaving behind the streets of Rosario, the people she loved, and the friends she had known since she was a kid. But when desire and chance come together, the way forward is clear. Leo took on the task, eager to start this new part of his journey. He was driven by his unwavering love of the game and the dreams he held close to his heart.

Training with the Best

As soon as Leo stepped foot on this strange land, he saw how different it was from his home city of Rosario and this busy European city. Everything was so different from what he was used to: the tall buildings, the confusing streets, the strange language that buzzed in his ears, and the variety of new foods. But even with all of these big changes, one thing stayed the same: the football field.

This huge area of green became Leo's safe place. Every morning, when he put on his shoes and walked out onto the field, homesickness and doubt would go away and be replaced by pure focus and drive. The training lessons were very hard and took all

of his energy. Still, Leo did well. With the help of experienced coaches who gave him important tips and strategies, he learned about techniques and styles that he had never seen in Argentina. He was also surrounded by a group of young, talented people, each of whom brought their own style to the game. They became friends, pushed each other, and took their games to new levels by working together.

Every day, Leo would train for hours and leave the field soaked in sweat but with a smile on his face. He was not only getting better at what he already did well, but he was also getting bigger, faster, and more confident as a player. And as the days turned into months, the once strange place started to feel a little more like home. This was all thanks to football, which brings people together.

The World Takes Notice

The world of sports is very big, and there are always a lot of talented people trying to stand out. But every once in a while, a star rises and gets the attention of fans, reviewers, and other players. Leo was going to become that star. As he played match after match and showed off his great skills, smooth moves, and amazing ability to read the game, his name started to get talked about in stadiums, fan groups, and football conversations.

His past problems with growing up became small details in a story that grew about a boy with unmatched ability and hard work. Every time he went out on the field, there was a noticeable energy, a buzzing excitement to see what magic Leo would do next. Every move, pass, and goal he made made him even more famous. Fans of football all over the world were seeing a genius come into his own, whether they had seen him play or had only heard stories about him.

From the busy streets of Rosario to the big stadiums of Europe, Leo's journey showed how powerful dreams, hard work, and love can be. No longer was he just a kid with a ball. He gave a lot of people hope because he showed that with heart and hard work, you can beat any obstacle and reach legendary heights in football.

This heartwarming tale draws inspiration from the life of Lionel Messi, a football icon who, despite health challenges in his early years, dared to dream of becoming a legend in the world of soccer.

CHAPTER 3: TOM'S LEAP OF FAITH

Every night, something magical happened in a cute neighborhood with streets lined with trees and houses with white picket fences. As the sun started to go down, it made long, playful shadows on the ground. In one backyard, the rhythmic thud of a soccer ball could be heard.

Young Tom played his heart out on this piece of grass. His gloves were worn out from making so many saves, and the goal post was made out of old wooden sticks and rope. His hard work was clear from the way he moved quickly from one side of the goal to the other and practiced every move with great care.

His eyes, which were full of dreams and fire, would light up every time he made a diving save or jumped high to catch a ball. When the sun was setting, it looked like he was channeling the souls of his favorite goalkeepers, the ones he watched on TV and wanted to be like one day.

<u>The Challenge No One Saw</u>

From the outside, Tom's life looked like it was full of simple childhood pleasures. His everyday soccer practice was surrounded by laughter, cheers when he saved a ball, and the soft hum of evening crickets. But when we looked more closely, we saw that Tom was facing a secret battle every day.

Tom had a health problem that made his body twitch and shake without notice, but not many people knew about it. It didn't hurt, and it didn't stop him from diving for a ball or telling his made-up friends what to do. Still, it had a more deep and personal effect. Every movement he couldn't help making was met with curious looks, whispered talks, or nudges and winks from kids his age. The playground could be both a place of happiness and a place where you have to work hard.

Even though he tried to hide how he felt by playing hard and smiling, the weight of the odd jokes and never-ending looks got to him. Every twitch was a reminder, and every whisper was a dagger. But Tom's love for soccer and his strong will often served as a shield, keeping the shadows of doubt away from his dreams and goals.

An Unwavering Spirit

Tom always knew where to go to get away from the problems and whispers: the soccer field. The green fields seemed to go on forever, bringing him to a place where he felt most like himself. With every step he took on the grass, the weight of his illness seemed to lighten. It was as if the field absorbed all his fears and let him be a normal boy who loved the game.

Tom wasn't just playing a game when he dove to block a hard shot or jumped into the air to catch a ball against a cloudy sky. He was telling a story about a boy who didn't let his problems define him. Every order he shouted to his friends and every strategy he came up with in the middle of a fast-paced game was his way of sending a quiet but strong message: that he was a force to be reckoned with, not because of his condition, but in spite of it.

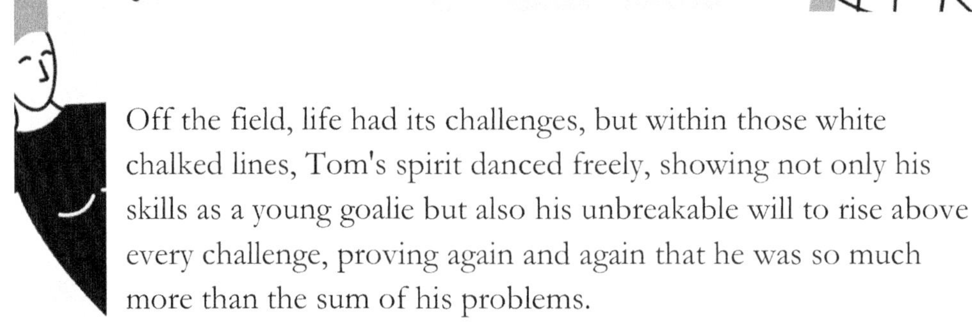

Off the field, life had its challenges, but within those white chalked lines, Tom's spirit danced freely, showing not only his skills as a young goalie but also his unbreakable will to rise above every challenge, proving again and again that he was so much more than the sum of his problems.

<u>The Coach with the Golden Advice</u>

Tom's coach called him over after a hard practice, when the sun was setting and most of the players were talking or going home. It wasn't like when they usually talked about strategy or gave him comments on his dives; the coach's eyes had a different look. He had watched Tom not only as a player but also as a young soul fighting an unseen storm. The coach did notice that the young boy's legs sometimes shook, but what really got his attention was his strong will and obvious skill between the goalposts.

Leaning in and speaking with the kind of gentle authority that only comes with years of experience, Tom's teacher said things that would change his way of thinking for years to come. "Tom," he said in a soft but strong voice, "I've seen players come and go, each fighting in their own way. But what makes a person special is not the lack of problems, but how they deal with them. After a short pause, he looked at Tom straight in the eyes to make sure he understood what he had said. "Use your problems as a stepping stone to get to where you want to be. Don't let them hold you back like a cage."

These words, which were whispered on a windy night when the smell of freshly cut grass was in the air, became a signpost for Tom. Not only were they about sports, but also about life in

general. In them, Tom found the affirmation and strength he needed to take on his journey and use every struggle as a step toward becoming great.

Triumph Over Trials

As the months went by and the seasons changed, people in the football world started to hear more and more about Tom. During games, people were amazed by his amazing jumps to the left and right. He often caught balls that looked impossible to catch. But even as his list of impressive saves grew, people weren't just talking about how good he was as a goalie. People in the stands talked about a young boy whose drive to overcome life's challenges was both inspiring and fascinating.

Local newspapers started to write about him. The stories weren't just about his sports stats, but also about his life. "The Keeper with Grit," one title said. Parents told their kids about him not just as a sports hero, but also as an example of what hard work could do. It didn't take long before teams from all over the area wanted him to be their last line of defense, not just because he was good at football but also because he brought a strong spirit to the team.

His love for soccer shone brightly, but it was the flame of drive inside him that never went out, even when things got hard, that made Tom's journey truly remarkable. He was no longer just a player; he had become a figure of overcoming difficulties.

Standing Tall

In the soccer world, people started talking about a young goalkeeper from a small town who had a knack for beating the chances. It wasn't just Tom's dives and saves that got people talking; it was the passion and hard work he put into everything he did. Soon, these whispers became loud conversations among the elite, and people at famous soccer academies heard about it.

Tom started getting invitations from top-tier academies. Each letter was marked with their logos and offered him scholarships and golden chances to improve his skill. They talked about advanced training programs, working with well-known teachers, and getting to play with some of the best young football players in the country. These were the dreams Tom had often thought about when he was practicing in the garden, and now they were coming true.

Tom took a deep breath. The sound of the leaves rustling reminded him of playing in the neighborhood, and his coach's words echoed in his mind. It was time to move on to bigger and better things. He took these offers and started a new part of his life, ready to improve his skills and stand taller in the face of difficulties.

An Inspiration for All

Young people who want to play soccer often tell the same story on soccer fields and training grounds. It's the story of Tom, a young boy from a nice neighborhood who danced around problems and used them to get closer to his goals. Coaches talk about his jumps, saves, and, most of all, his unbreakable spirit with a sparkle in their eyes.

People talk about how Tom didn't just play soccer, he lived it. They say this in the huddles after practice or during the break talks. Even though the ground was shaking and people were talking, he kept his mind on the roar of the crowd, the thrill of making a save, and the fun of the game. His story showed that challenges can be turned into chances if you have determination, grit, and a strong love for what you do.

As new players put on their shoes and take their places, they can't help but think about Tom. They are told that the road to success is often full of obstacles, but that anyone can become an example with the right attitude and drive. Tom's story of how he went from that small backyard to top academies is more than just a soccer story. It's a lesson in perseverance, hope, and the amazing power of believing in yourself.

In the spirit of Tom Heaton, this story showcases how a young star goalkeeper overcame medical obstacles to prove that even adversity couldn't hinder his path to success.

CHAPTER 4: SARA'S SURPRISE WIN

In a quaint beach town, the gentle breeze always carried a hint of salt, and the sun seemed to cast a special golden glow that made everything just a bit brighter. The town's heart was beating the fastest at the playground, where the sounds of children laughing and waves breaking could be heard. Sara was one of the kids in the crowd. She was a lively girl with a spirit as wild as the wind. With every wind gust, her hair would dance, showing how free-spirited she was.

Most of the kids on the playground were enchanted by soccer and chased balls around with joy, but Sara was a lovely exception. She was often seen handling a different kind of ball than a soccer ball. This ball held the history of her family. She didn't just see it as a game; it was a treasured custom that had been passed down to her with love. Every bounce and move she made reminded me of family get-togethers, old stories, and how much fun it was to play that sport together.

But in the middle of all the soccer yells and children's fun chatter, Sara's unique game stood out as a fascinating sight. It showed how many different cultures and traditions the town had, and Sara, with her unique ball and skills, was its bright symbol.

<u>A chance game</u>

One sunny afternoon, Sara was playing her favorite sport with her special ball when she made a mistake that caused it to bounce away from her. It rolled and spun around until it stopped in the middle of a group of excited kids playing soccer. They watched as the strange ball stopped their game, and when they looked at the ball's owner, there was an offer in the air. "Why don't you join us for a round?" they all asked at the same time.

Sara paused and looked down at her shoes, which weren't quite made for soccer's sharp turns and turns. She thought back to the last time she played the sport, which made her realize how strange it was. Still, the group's excitement, smiles, and fun nudges to join them made her heart beat faster. Maybe it was the excitement of the moment, or maybe she just wanted to try something that was just a little bit outside of her comfort zone. She thought, "Why not?" with a shrug and a smile. After all, it's just one game." And then she took her place among them.

What Comes Naturally

The whistle went off, which meant the start of the friendly match. But as the minutes went by, something amazing started to happen. Every time Sara touched or moved, she showed a unique speed and quickness that caught her opponents by surprise. It was clear that her quick footwork, quick movements, and natural sense of space, which she had developed in her previous sport, helped her on the soccer field. Even though the stage was different, she did each move as if she were dancing a pattern she had done for years.

Her friends looked at her, first in shock and then in pure awe. Opponents couldn't guess what she would do next, and her teammates quickly learned to trust her with the ball after seeing how easily she threaded passes and dodged hits. The game, which started out as something fun to do on the spot, quickly turned into a show, with Sara at its heart.

The game was over when the final whistle blew, but the excitement didn't go away. There was a buzz in the air, a mix of awe and excitement. Sara's friends crowded around her and gave her compliments and acted like they didn't believe her. They would ask, "Where did that come from?" with laughter and surprise in their voices. To them, the girl who came from a world where a different ball sport was played was now the brightest star on their soccer field. She showed that different starts can sometimes lead to unexpected successes.

Getting ready for the new challenge

People in the beach town started to talk about Sara's new skills on the playgrounds and in the fields. As the days turned into weeks, Sara was caught between two worlds. Her heart was pulled between the sport her family had played for generations and the excitement of soccer. Each had its own special appeal: the beloved tradition and memories tied to her first sport, and the exhilarating teamwork she felt when she played soccer. Both worlds came together in a way that made sense as she raced across different fields, using what she learned in one to do better in the other.

The committed soccer coach in the town heard about Sara's ability to change and adapt. He was interested, so he went to see one of the informal games she played in. As he watched her fluid movements, sharp instincts, and unwavering drive, he saw more

than just a good player. He saw a lot of potential that needed to be developed. It was only reasonable to invite Sara to join the best youth soccer team in the town. And Sara was excited about the chance to improve her skills and play at a higher level, so she jumped at the chance.

Star Shooting on the Field

Time has a way of making interests stronger, and as the months turned into years, Sara's dedication to soccer became stronger and stronger. She trained hard in the mornings and nights, often under a blanket of sparkling stars or the first light of dawn. As she learned more about the game, she picked up strategies, mastered skills, and looked for ways to improve her play. The speed and quick footwork she had learned in her previous sport now worked well with the soccer skills she had just learned, giving her a style of play that was all her own.

It didn't take long for her skills to show on the field. Sara's ability to get through defenders and find the back of the net got better and better with each game, making her the most important player on her team. The fact that she was good at more than one sport made her unreliable and dangerous. Each of her goals, which she scored with skill and precision, not only added to the score but also won her praise. People began to talk about Sara's achievements outside of their town, and many called her the "shooting star" of the soccer field.

From the coast to the stage of the world

Sara's trip began in the salty air of her hometown on the coast, but it soon caught the attention of places far away. The word

about her amazing skills spread like wildfire, reaching far beyond her seaside neighborhood. Invitations started coming in from the best soccer schools, all of which wanted to train and show off the child prodigy they had heard about. Sara took on these new tasks and chances with the same enthusiasm she showed on her neighborhood playground. In no time, she was wearing the colors of her country, playing on national stages, and stunning people with her unmatched skill.

Her rapid rise in soccer wasn't just a sign of how good she was; it was also a sign of how brave she was to change her dreams. The girl who used to chase a different ball around her neighborhood while kids played around her was now a role model on the big football stage. Sara was more than just a soccer star to many people. She became a symbol of the power of breaking rules, of going beyond what's comfortable, and of the endless possibilities that come with daring to dream outside the box.

This chapter takes inspiration from the journey of Sara Däbritz, whose transition from another sport to soccer led to unexpected stardom and remarkable achievements.

CHAPTER 5: MOE'S RACE AGAINST TIME

Moe found his calling in a small, rural town where the green fields seemed to go on forever and the roads wound around each other like a complicated puzzle. Every morning, when the sky was just beginning to get light, he was already out there, in an open area. With every kick, run, and twist and turn of his foot, he wasn't just playing the game; he was one with it.

This open space wasn't just another piece of land in the town. For Moe, it was holy ground and his safe place. To someone who wasn't paying attention, it might have just looked like a boy playing a game. Moe, on the other hand, saw every moment on the field as a lesson, a task, and a chance. His passion for sports was so strong that it could be felt and drew other people to him. Children would gather around with wide-eyed wonder, hoping to learn a trick or two, while the older villagers stood back and watched with looks of both respect and pride on their faces.

Moe couldn't get state-of-the-art facilities or expert coaching in the town because it didn't have enough money. But it made up for what it didn't have with spirit and friendship. Moe's love for the game didn't fade in this setting. Instead, it grew stronger, fueled by his dreams and the hopes of the whole group.

Whispers of a Prodigy

People started to hear about Moe's amazing skills far beyond the green fields and winding paths of his town. It seemed like every gust of wind and every bird's song told a story about his amazing skills. Visitors to the town, whether they were there for business, for fun, or just to pass through, always talked about this young player. People talked about how amazing it was that he could make the ball dance to his music as if it were an extension of his own body.

When teams from other villages or towns came to play, they would not only remember the game, but they would also tell amazing stories about Moe. There were stories about how he dribbled past multiple players like they were just training cones, how his shots hit their targets with uncanny accuracy, and how he seemed to have a footballing sense that was much older than his years. When these stories were told over and over again, he became something of a neighborhood legend.

But to the people in his town, Moe was more than just a genius or a legend. He was the personification of dreams, goals, and, most of all, hope. Every goal he scored and every skillful touch he made showed that fame can come from the most humble beginnings. Moe wasn't just their best player; he was also a lighthouse that showed others the way.

A Chance Encounter

One sunny afternoon, when everyone in the village was watching a game that everyone was looking forward to, a new face joined the crowd. This man was a scout from a well-known city club. He had a good eye and acted like he had spent his whole life playing football. He had heard about Moe's amazing skills, so he went to see the village genius in action. He was interested in finding a new talent, so he went to see Moe perform.

As the games went on, it became clear that the stories weren't just a bunch of lies. Moe was the best player on the field. He planned plays and played with the kind of skill you'd expect from players who went to top academies. Every move, every pass, and every goal showed a skill that was raw and brilliant at the same time. As soon as the final whistle blew, the scout knew he had found something special. He went up to Moe right away and offered him a golden chance: he could train in the city with world-class equipment and coaches, which would help him improve his skills and move up in the professional football world.

From Village Grounds to City Lights

As soon as Moe entered the city, he saw a scene that was very different from his town. Skyscrapers touched the sky, cars honked nonstop, and huge crowds of people walked through the busy streets, making a symphony of city life. Every part of the city seemed to be full of life, energy, and plans. But in spite of all the changes, the young village prodigy's heart stayed the same. Soccer was still his compass, his leading light.

Moe was amazed by how well-equipped the city's training sites were. Unlike the rough village fields, these turfs were well-kept, had the latest equipment, and were surrounded by trainers with a

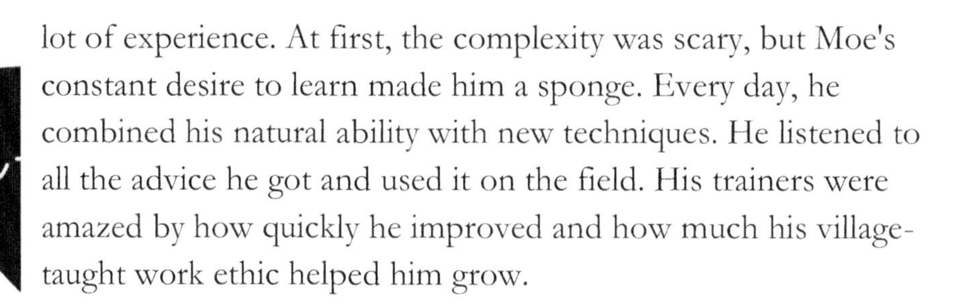

lot of experience. At first, the complexity was scary, but Moe's constant desire to learn made him a sponge. Every day, he combined his natural ability with new techniques. He listened to all the advice he got and used it on the field. His trainers were amazed by how quickly he improved and how much his village-taught work ethic helped him grow.

But not just the game needed to be changed. Living in the city came with its own problems. The speed, the way of life, and the sheer size of everything were sometimes too much to handle. Still, Moe's strength showed through. He used the same drive that got him up at dawn in his town every day to train, pushing himself harder and harder as the days went by. His past didn't hold him back; instead, it made him stronger. It reminded him of where he came from and gave him the drive to do well in the big city.

Europe Beckons

Moe's skills on the field didn't just make waves in his home country; they reverberated across countries and caught the attention of scouts in Europe. After seeing the best talent in the world, these scouts were always looking for the next big thing. When they heard that a small town had a very talented person, they were naturally interested. When they watched him play, they were amazed by how well he handled the ball and how sharp his skills were on the field. Moe wasn't just another player with potential; he was a gem that needed to be polished.

Offers from well-known clubs in Europe started coming in, and each one was more tempting than the last. They made up stories about Moe wearing their jerseys and playing under bright lights in arenas full of cheering fans. Every soccer player's dream was to

play on those hallowed fields with soccer stars. Moe's rise was nothing short of meteoric. He went from playing on the simple, peaceful fields of his village, where his love was born, to having the chance to play on the hallowed grounds of Europe. His story wasn't just about soccer; it was a tribute to a spirit that never gave up and a love that never died.

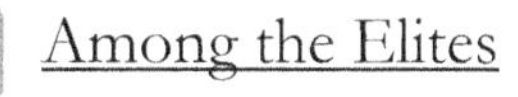

Among the Elites

Moe's presence on the biggest football stages in Europe showed how strong dreams and unwavering drive can be. With each game he played and each skillful move and smart move, he became more than just another player on the field. He became a role model for many young people from poor homes, showing them that their dreams, no matter how big, could be reached. His story hit home with a lot of people, especially those who had to deal with problems and had few resources. It reminded them that fire, grit, and a never-give-up attitude often win out over circumstances.

Moe stood out, but not just because of how good he was on the field. His story, about how he went from a small village to an elite sports stadium, gave his legend an extra layer. Every goal he scored and every award he won carried the weight of his past and the hopes of the people he helped. In the top levels of football, where many stories start with a nice place to train, Moe's story was a welcome change. He was a live proof that no dream is unreachable and no path is too hard for someone who is really passionate about something.

Moe's story reflects the dedication and skill of Mohamed Salah, whose journey from a humble village to the grand stages of European football serves as a testament to his relentless pursuit of excellence.

CHAPTER 6: CHRISTIE'S TEAM SPIRIT

Soccer has a special place in the hearts of the people who live in Canada's vast regions, where snow-capped mountains touch the sky and vast prairies go on forever. This country, with its many different cultures and beautiful landscapes, has adopted the sport not just as a hobby but also as a way to bring people together. It brings together different groups of people, each with their own stories, under the same flag of love for the "beautiful game."

Christie stood out against this background of soccer excitement. Her raven-black hair, which she often wore in a tight bun, became a symbol of hard work, and her sharp eyes showed that she was a fierce athlete who wouldn't settle for anything less than the best. On the field, her skill with the ball was clear, and people in the stands cheered and clapped. But more than her individual skills, what really set Christie apart was her natural ability to rally her team and make them feel like they were unbeatable when they worked together.

The Heart of the Team

There are stars on every team whose names fans chant and whose every move on the field is closely watched. They are the ones whose goals are shown over and over again, and whose fans wear their outfits. Behind all of this glitz and glamor, though, there are unsung heroes whose contributions aren't always summed up in numbers or highlight reels. They are the team's heartbeats and the glue that holds everyone together, making sure that the team spirit doesn't break.

Christie was an unusual mix of these two worlds. Because of her amazing skill, she was often in the spotlight, and her amazing goals and perfect plays were often the focus of post-game analysis. Her name was sung together by tens of thousands of fans in the arenas. But he was more than just a star. He was a guide and an anchor. Christie had an amazing sense of how people felt in the locker room. She would be the first to talk to a partner who seemed off and give them a hug or a pat on the back. She was a guide for the new players, and when things got tough, her words would ring out during halftime, giving her teammates hope and a boost of energy. For her, it wasn't just about the game; it was about the team family she had made.

Challenges and Triumphs

The Canadian national team didn't have an easy time getting where they are now. As they moved through the complex world of international soccer, they met teams whose skills and plans often seemed to be in a different league. These enemies were a big problem because they had their own histories of wins and traditions. There were times when the shirt, which stood for their country's hopes and dreams, felt like it was almost too heavy to carry. Some doubts crept in, and the whispers of those who didn't believe got louder with every mistake.

Christie, on the other hand, never stopped being a model of strength. She stepped up when she saw that waves of uncertainty were sometimes shaking the team to its core. Every time she gave them a pep talk, she reminded them of the fights they had won and the hard times they had been through to be able to wear that jersey. It wasn't about taking on the soccer "giants," but about remembering who they were and how strong they were when they worked together.

Under Christie's direction, the team started to see past the problems they were facing right then. They started playing not only as good players but also as a family with a common goal. Every pass, every goal, and every save became a sign of their team unity. Christie made sure that even though the world saw them as eleven different people, they went out on the field as one heart and one soul, with an unbreakable bond and a common goal.

Victory Beyond the Goals

With Christie in charge, the Canadian team won a lot of games, and each one was bigger and better than the last. But, as great as the scores and prizes were, they only told part of their story. Behind the scenes, away from the noise of the crowds and the bright lights of the stadium, a deeper link was made. The players didn't just pass the ball to their friends; they also gave it to their sisters. Not only did they all want the same thing, but they also spent a lot of time together laughing, consoling each other after a tough loss, and getting to know each other as players and people. This is what made them a team.

This deep friendship went beyond what happened on the soccer field. The world might have thought that their choreographed moves, perfect teamwork, and trust in each other during games were the result of hard training. But those who knew knew that it was also the result of real love and a deep sense of friendship. Their wins weren't just about how many goals they scored, but

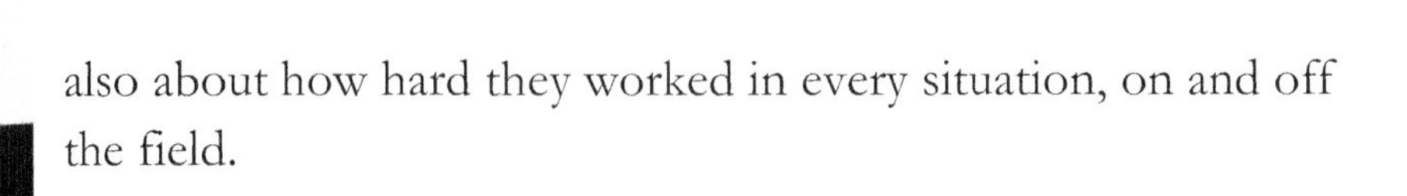

also about how hard they worked in every situation, on and off the field.

Legacy of Unity

Time's ebbs and flows brought new players to the Canadian national team every season, but Christie's mark on the team's core values never went away. People loved to talk about her amazing goals and masterful moves on the field, but it was the strong team spirit she built that became the most important part of her memory. Even after she left the field, her lessons and the ideals she taught continued to show up in every pass, goal, and celebration. The teamwork and togetherness she pushed for were no longer just things that a team did; they became a part of the way Canadian soccer was made.

For people my age and younger, Christie was more than just a sports star. As they watched from the stands, their eyes were wide with awe and their hearts were full of hopes. They saw her as a shining example of how to be a leader. Not only was she good with the ball, but she could also bring people together and make them feel better. In Christie, they found not only a player to look up to, but also a leader to try to be like. Christie knew that a team's strength came from its spirit as well as its skills.

Inspired by the leadership of Christine Sinclair, this chapter explores how her team spirit uplifted her national team, leading them to remarkable success on the soccer field.

CHAPTER 7: NATE'S SMILE AND HUSTLE

Children's laughter filled a small, friendly town every day, and the streets were full of bicycles that kids had carelessly left behind while they were too busy playing. Nate's first real love was soccer, which he found in this town. It was a golden summer afternoon, and crickets were chirping in the evening.

His small garden with patches of wildflowers and an old, crooked tree in the way became his own soccer haven. He would often use the tree's crooked branches as goal posts, and the light coming through the tree's leaves would light up his homemade field. Every time Nate sent the ball flying with a happy kick, his bright blue shoes left soft marks on the grassy carpet. This was a quiet record of how he went from just daydreaming about amazing goals to becoming an expert at scoring them.

The sound of the ball hitting the tree or bouncing off the fence became familiar as it happened every day. Each echo was a sign of how hard Nate worked, showing how he went from being a young boy with hopes to a promising player whose eyes shone with determination.

<u>A Smile that Won Hearts</u>

Every day, when the sun started to go down and throw a warm golden blanket over the town, Nate couldn't wait to put on his shoes and head to the soccer field. The sound of children practicing their kicks and joking around filled the field, which was

surrounded by tall pine trees and daisies that swayed in the evening breeze. Nate stood out among them. Not only for his quick feet and ability to read the game, but also for something much more heartwarming: his constant smile.

Nate's face was always lit up with a bright, steady smile, whether the ball went into the net or missed it. When his shots were perfect, his smile showed that he was happy and proud of himself. When things didn't go as planned, it was a sign of his unwavering positivity and told the world that he'd just try again. Nate was liked by his peers and teachers right away because he was strong and happy at the same time.

But what drew people to him wasn't just his skill or even that smile. It was the way that smile made her feel. Nate's positive attitude would often lift up kids, adults, coworkers, and even rivals. His appearance on the field was a reminder that soccer was really about happiness, friendship, and the thrill of the game itself. Soon, everyone in town started to love Nate not just because he was a good player, but also because he had become a symbol of hope and happiness.

The Town's Little Champion

On a bright morning, there was a lot of excitement in a nearby field. The yearly soccer tournament in the town was going on, and the stands were full of excited people cheering and laughing to show their support. Nate's team was playing against their toughest foes. They were a lively group with jerseys that all had stripes. As the first half went on, the other team's defenders let two goals through. Nate's teammates all had worried looks on their faces, which were a mix of sadness and worry. You could feel how tense things were.

But in the middle of all the stress, Nate was the only one who could stay cool. His smile, which was always there, seemed to shine even brighter during that hard time. "Hey, team!" he yelled, and his friends crowded around him. "Don't forget why we play. Because it's fun, we like each other, and we love the game. We can do it!" His words were like magic because they were full of real belief and hope. With a nod and a cheer, the team went back to their places with renewed energy.

Nate was all over the field. He playfully dribbled past players, set up beautiful passes, and led the team's moves with the grace of a maestro. The change in mood was clear. Every time Nate scored a goal, the crowd cheered and he gave his trademark bright-eyed smile. What looked like a sure loss turned into a show of strength and teamwork, led by Nate. This showed that sometimes, a little bit of optimism can turn the tide.

The Big City Opportunity

In the center of the town, stories about how good Nate was at soccer became part of the local lore. More than his ability, though, what really stood out was his warm smile that was always there. It seemed like his love for the game spread far beyond the borders of the town, attracting the attention of people whose job it is to find the next big soccer star.

Nate got a thick letter from a well-known sports school in the big city one day. It had the school's logo on it. There was an invite inside. The school had heard about Nate's skill on the field and how happy he made everyone feel. They thought he was not only a good player but also a great representative of the sport. They offered him a place at their school, where he would get excellent training and meet some of the best young players in the country.

The chance to do something was huge. As Nate packed his soccer shoes, shin guards, and some of his favorite snacks, the air was filled with a mix of joy and nervousness. Nate gave his parents his signature smile as he stood on the train platform. The skyline of the big city was just a few stops away. It was a smile that told them, "It's a big step, but I'm ready."

City Lights, Same Bright Smile

Nate found himself in a completely different world in the middle of the huge city, with its tall buildings and busy streets. Under the lights of the city, the soccer fields got bigger and greener, and the air was full of the drive of young players who wanted to make their mark. The training classes were hard, and every player was pushed to their limits with drills that required their full attention and skill.

Still, Nate's spirit stayed the same through all of these changes. He was just as fiery about the game, and his always-present smile was just as warm. After a hard drill, he was the one to give a tired partner a hand or say something positive to keep the mood up. Outside of the field, he never missed a chance to do something nice. Nate's heart was always in the right place, whether he was helping a fellow player with their gear, sharing his snacks, or getting an extra water bottle for someone during a break.

People in the city didn't have to wait long to notice the bright spot that Nate brought with him. Everyone liked him right away, from the experienced coaches to the young fans who came to watch their practices. He had a lot of raw ability, worked hard all the time, and was always happy. Nate's smile stood out the most in a city full of bright lights.

Dreams Turn to Reality

In the big world of sports, Nate faced new problems every day, but he was always determined to solve them. The first thing he did in the morning was put on his bright blue sneakers and set new goals. These weren't just the kind of goals you score in a net, but also the ones that shaped his hopes. Every time he practiced, he pushed himself to his limits, learned new ways to dribble, and improved his tactics. But Nate liked soccer for more than just the way to play it. It was a dance that showed emotion, heart, and the value of working as a team.

People started to hear about this young player who was so talented and always played with a smile. With their sharp eyes, professional scouts saw more than just a skilled football player in Nate. They saw a shining example of good sportsmanship. Top teams heard about his ability, and it didn't take long for them to contact him. When the news got to his hometown, it made everyone happy. Nate's favorite happy face and a soccer ball were on a special cake made by a bakery in the area. Their young star was about to play in the big lights.

Nate felt the weight of the moment as he walked onto the huge competitive field. The stadium was huge, and there were a lot of people watching. Every seat was full of people who were excitedly

waiting. Even with all the cheering and cameras flashing, Nate's attitude stayed the same. He still played with the same joy, humility, and, of course, that smile. For him, the trip from the backyard to the big stadium showed how love and hard work can make dreams come true.

Nate's story takes cues from Neymar Jr., whose rapid ascent in professional soccer was marked not only by his extraordinary skills but also by his unwavering humility and heartwarming smile.

CHAPTER 8: SURESH'S DREAM FOR INDIA

In the lively center of India, children often flew colored kites from rooftops and balconies, making the skies dance. Narrow streets were full of people, and the smell of spicy curries wafted out of open windows, mixing with the sounds of laughing and talking. Suresh went to a dusty field, which became his soccer heaven every night, to get away from all the noise.

His favorite soccer ball told stories of all the games and adventures he had with it. It looked like a quilted fabric of memories because it was made of old pieces that had seen better days. Still, this ball meant more to Suresh than just the games it had been in. It was a reflection of his dreams. Dreams as big and colorful as the kites in the sky, full of hope and held together with a strong desire.

Suresh would stop for a moment every evening as the sun started to go down, painting the world in shades of gold and amber. He would lay down on the slightly worn-down grass and let the coolness of it soak into him. When he looked up, his eyes would get stuck on the vast span of the starry sky. He would imagine himself playing in huge stadiums under those stars, with roaring crowds cheering him on. Suresh believed with all his heart in this dream, which was as big as the sky.

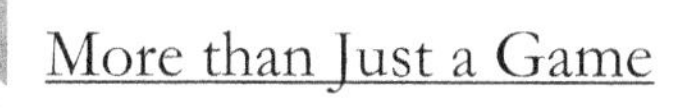

More than Just a Game

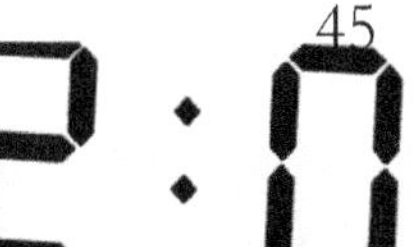

The steady thumping of a cricket ball and the cheers for a goal were well-known noises throughout India. The unquestioned favorite and a national obsession that brought people from all walks of life together was cricket. However, for Suresh, a different tune called to him: the thud of a soccer ball against his foot and the thrilling rush of sprinting through a field as the wind whipped past.

Soccer meant much more to Suresh than just sprinting and scoring goals. It symbolized a goal and a hope for his entire country as well as for himself. He perceived the importance and weight of the shirt he was wearing as a badge of honor rather than a burden. He participated in soccer matches for young boys in small towns, for children in packed city streets, and for any Indian who saw the sport's latent potential for their country.

Suresh wasn't just playing a game with each tenacious dash and each deft move. He was creating a message for his compatriots, urging them to understand and appreciate soccer's allure. He had faith in the game's charm, the sense of community it promoted, and India's ability to triumph on the world stage. And he was getting a little bit closer to making that belief a reality with each goal he scored.

A Nation's Hope on Young Shoulders

Soon, Suresh's name was being talked about by everyone. What started as whispers turned into excited talk, and stories turned into legends. His soccer career went from the dusty fields of his hometown to the well-kept fields of the best facilities in the country. As it did, the dreams of many people rose.

It wasn't easy to get on the national youth team. It meant harder training, learning from coaches with more experience, and most of all, living up to the standards of a whole country. When he put on the jersey with the three-color badge, he wasn't just putting on a piece of clothing. He was also putting on hope, ambition, and goals that had no limits. Every pass he made, goal he scored, and stop he made showed his dedication not only to the game but also to his country.

But Suresh didn't give up or lose focus, even though he was under a lot of pressure. Instead, he took it in stride. He understood that he wasn't just a player on a field; he was a symbol of hope for a billion people. Each game was a chance to get India closer to its proper place on the world soccer stage, not for personal glory but to move the country forward as a whole. Young people carried the hopes of a whole country, and Suresh was determined to help them fly.

The World Takes Notice

The mood in the big stadiums where international soccer was played was electric. The world's most popular sport was a colorful tapestry of packed arenas, cheering crowds, and waving flags from all over the world. The games were a mix of different cultures, with each team bringing their own style, strategies, and years of history to the field. In this mix of soccer from all over the world, a young player from India began to stand out.

Suresh had a very clear style. Every move he made, whether it was a smart dribble, a quick pass, or a strong shot, he did with beauty and accuracy. He played with so much energy and emotion that it was hard to look away. Soccer fans, reporters, and even the teams they were playing noticed. Soon, articles in newspapers and magazines around the world had big headlines about the young genius from India. "Keep an eye on Suresh from India; he's a rising star!" said seasoned commentators, whose voices could be heard in the stadiums.

But for Suresh, it was about more than just himself. Every time he went out on the field, he brought the pride and dreams of his country with him. With every goal he scored and award he won, he not only made himself better known, but also raised the standing of Indian soccer on the world stage. The message was clear and strong: India was no longer just an up-and-coming soccer team; thanks to the goals and hard work of young Suresh, it had firmly established itself in the world soccer scene.

A Legacy in the Making

As the months turned on the calendar, something beautiful started to happen in India. People started building soccer fields in places you wouldn't expect, like in the middle of huge cities, next to peaceful rivers in the country, and even on top of mountains. Suresh's never-ending dedication and unmatched success on the world stage had sparked a wave of soccer excitement across the country. Once the most common sound, the crack of a cricket bat now blends with the thud of soccer balls being kicked in alleyways, parks, and open fields.

Young kids started trading their cricket gear for soccer jerseys and shoes because they wanted to play soccer. They saw in Suresh a way to reach their own dreams, a light showing them that with hard work and drive, they too could reach the stars. The story was changing. People now talked about Suresh's most recent games, his goals, and the hope he gave to a country that wanted to be known for its soccer around the world.

Every time Suresh played a game in a foreign stadium, he felt the weight and warmth of his country's hopes. As the Indian national song played and millions of people sang along from their homes, he had a profound realization. The goal he had for himself had become a goal for everyone. Every goal and win sent the same word to the rest of the world: "India isn't just here to play. India is here to fight, to inspire, and to leave a mark on the world of soccer."

This chapter is inspired by the ambition and talent of Sunil Chhetri, who dedicated himself to earning recognition for his nation in the world of football.

CHAPTER 9: HOPE IN THE FIELD: ZARA'S SQUAD

In a place with tall mountains that reached to the sky and wide plains that looked like the pages of an old story, there was a simple field. It wasn't a lush green field with a perfectly even surface. The land was rough, and the grass was often broken up. But Zara and her group of friends thought of it as their own little piece of paradise. For them, its flaws made it even more special and showed how far they had come on their own trip.

When the first rays of sunshine came through the mountain peaks each morning, they gave the valley a golden color. This magic of dawn that changed things was always accompanied by a steady thud. It sounded like a soccer ball was being hit, passed, and sometimes missed. But the sound was always the same, like a heartbeat in the emptiness of the landscape, whether the fish found the net or not.

The sound of the ball hitting the ground wasn't just a sound. It was full of hopes, dreams, and a strong will. It was full of stories of hope and of being strong. Every kick, pass, goal, and miss had a story to tell. A story about young people who find their voice, their passion, and, most of all, their shared dream in the huge mountains.

Zara led the way. Her long braids were tied with bright ribbons. Each person on her team had her own style and personality, but they all worked toward the same goal. Even though their shirts didn't match, they wore them with pride. Every practice was full

of laughs, jokes, and the pure joy of playing the game. The sight of these little girls playing so hard in the middle of the vast Afghan countryside was nothing short of magical.

A Beacon of Inspiration

In the middle of rough terrain, the team was more than just a group of girls who played soccer. They were a united front that showed what could be done when people worked together toward the same goal. Every training session, every game, and every goal showed how determined they were as a team. The soccer field was Zara and her friends' canvas, and with each game, they painted a vivid picture of hard work and determination.

Their story was heard far beyond the limits of their field. It sent a strong message to their community and the rest of the world, showing that ideas could grow even in the most difficult places. Every time they went out on the field, they didn't just play for fun. They played for a much bigger reason. They played for every young dreamer, but especially for the girls who were told their goals were too high or out of reach.

Zara's team didn't just play soccer, though. Every time they played, they broke down old rules and made new ones. They were pioneers who broke stereotypes and set new standards. Their story wasn't just about how happy they were when they scored or how sad they were when they missed. It was a story of courage, hope, and, most of all, young people who were willing to change their lives.

Victory Beyond Scores

Every time the ball was passed, a shot was taken at the goal, or a player ran across the field, it showed how strong they were. The final scores of each game? They didn't mean anything. What really counted were the laughs, the shared moments of success, and even the tears of disappointment that came from time to time. For these girls, the fun wasn't just in winning, but in playing the game itself.

Bonds that can't be broken on the field

Every time they played a game, something magical would happen. There was a deeper link being made that went beyond the plans and the goals. The girls weren't just teammates; they were also close friends with a common goal. As they got together, made plans, and cheered each other on, they made memories that would last a lifetime. The real victories of their trip were the times when they whispered words of encouragement to each other, cheered as a group, or even sighed together after a missed chance.

Zara's team's soccer field was a place of hope in the vast landscapes of Afghanistan, where life often brought a lot of problems. Here, among the cheers and friendly hits, they were able to forget about the problems they faced every day. But more than that, they came to be seen as signs of strength. Their message was clear and loud: no matter where you come from, if you have heart and determination, you can make your dreams come true. These young girls showed how powerful hope is and how beautiful it is to find joy in the little things through soccer.

Drawing inspiration from the passion and determination of Nadia Nadim, this chapter tells the story of Zara and her team of young girls, representing their undying love for soccer even in challenging terrains.

2:0

CHAPTER 10: THE NORDIC SURPRISE

In a remote part of the world, a white layer of snow covered the land for most of the year. Here, winters lasted longer, spreading their icy fingers across the land, and the Northern Lights put on a magical show, dancing and weaving bright colors across the vast night sky. People in this Nordic area were strong and tough. Their spirits shone as brightly as the Northern Lights, and neither the cold nor the night could dim them.

This small country didn't have a lot of land, but its heart and drive were huge. Its people loved their old practices, enjoyed the beauty of their ice-covered fjords and tall mountain peaks, and had a deep love for soccer. On any given day, you could see kids playing lively soccer games on the peaceful white plains. They would run after patched-up soccer balls on snow-covered fields while wearing lots of warm clothes. Their rosy faces would show through their scarves and hats. The sound of their happy laughter would rise and melt into the cold air.

The freezing cold didn't stop these young people from loving the game. Instead, it became a big part of how they played, teaching them to be tough and giving their games a unique twist. In this country, where the weather often tried to bring people down, soccer showed how passionate and determined they were.

A Team Like No Other

Many people thought they were the losers because they came from a place where soccer fields were covered in snow for a large part of the year. But it was this setting that gave them the strength to survive. They didn't let the harsh weather and icy landscapes stop them. Instead, they used them to fuel their fierce drive.

Their training wasn't just about getting better at skills or improving moves. It was about fighting against the weather, taking control of the snow-covered fields, and making every gust of cold wind into a lesson in staying strong. In their home country, where it was cold, they had to work harder than usual. It took a strong will and a burning desire that was strong enough to keep the cold away. When they practiced, they didn't just work on their bodies; they also strengthened their hearts. This made them ready to face any task, on or off the field.

When they went out on the world stage, they brought with them the strength, persistence, and spirit of their home country. Many times, their opponents, who were usually from bigger countries with long sports histories, would think they were better than they were. But with every game, this team would show that it's not the size of the country that counts, but the heart of its players. Their amazing mix of skill, planning, and a strong desire to win left many of their famous opponents not only defeated, but also very impressed.

Lighting Up the World Stage

The world's best soccer tournament was in full swing, and this team, far from their cold home country, stepped onto the field not just to play, but to enchant. Every time they played, they

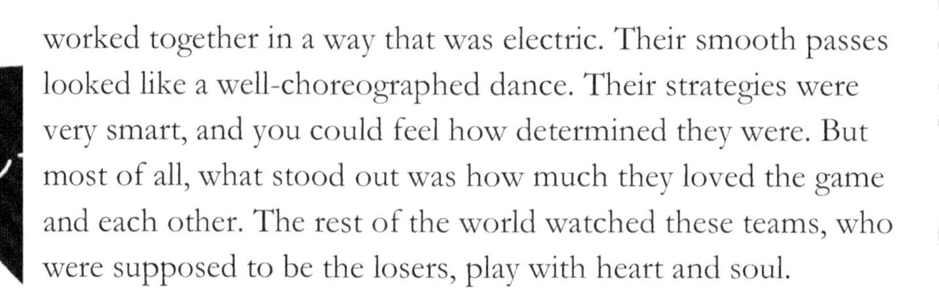

worked together in a way that was electric. Their smooth passes looked like a well-choreographed dance. Their strategies were very smart, and you could feel how determined they were. But most of all, what stood out was how much they loved the game and each other. The rest of the world watched these teams, who were supposed to be the losers, play with heart and soul.

As the game went on, whispers turned into loud cheers. "Have you seen the Nordic team play?" was a question that was asked often. Fans of football and people who had never played before were impressed not only by how well they played, but also by how hard they worked. They went against the odds by taking on giants with a strong will. Every goal they scored and every smart move they made was heard a long way from the stadium. They were the ultimate underdogs, showing that with drive and teamwork, even the biggest problems could be faced head-on. Even though they didn't win the final battle, their whole trip was a success.

The story of this small country in the north became a sign of hope and inspiration. At the end of the competition, they had made a mark that would never be forgotten. They hadn't just played soccer; they'd also told a story about determination, passion, and the power of confidence. Their story was a powerful reminder to everyone that real success isn't always about winning, but about the path and the people whose lives you change along the way. The world had seen a soccer story like no other and learned that a team's emotion and spirit on the field are more important than its size or height.

This chapter is inspired by the small Nordic nation that, against all odds, illuminated the world football stage with their spirit and talent, much like the Iceland national team.

CHAPTER 11: LEE'S EASTERN AMBITION

Lee's story started in the middle of a busy city, where tall buildings seemed to reach for the clouds and neon lights danced through the night. As the sky turned orange and purple at dawn, when most people in the city were still sleeping, Lee was already running around on the soccer field. The morning mist would stand still and watch as he moved gracefully between the cones, making sure that each step and move had a reason.

His routine was like a beat set against the sounds of birds waking up and the first trains going by in the distance. Lee worked on his kicks in a focused and controlled way, making the ball a part of himself. He would handle it with skill, sometimes letting it fly high and other times moving it with short, quick passes. He could barely hear the noise and bustle of the city waking up because his heartbeat was in sync with his thoughts.

With its dewy grass and ringing goals, that soccer field was more than just an open area in the middle of a city. It was a safe place for Lee. A canvas on which he drew his goals one focused kick at a time. Here, he gave life to his ideas and built a picture of the future with each sunrise practice.

<u>Bridging Two Worlds</u>

In Lee's homeland, soccer wasn't just a sport; it was a heartbeat that resonated through the streets and alleyways, echoed in the shouts of children and the cheers of avid fans. But despite its deep-rooted love for the game, there was an evident divide. The international football giants, with their celebrated histories and star-studded teams, seemed a world apart from the budding talent of Asian teams. The disparity was not just in skill, but also in the approach, strategy, and even the rhythm of play.

Yet, Lee was never one to shy away from a challenge. He saw this divide not as a hurdle, but as an opportunity—a chance to meld the best of both worlds. Nights would find him curled up, eyes glued to the screen, as he watched matches from every corner of the globe. From the energetic Latin American teams with their impeccable footwork to the disciplined European squads with their strategic plays, Lee was a sponge. He studied every pass, every move, every strategy. He noted the flair of the West and the discipline of the East, understanding that the fusion of both could be the secret to success.

With a heart full of ambition and a mind armed with global soccer insights, Lee began to practice what he had learned. He became a bridge between two worlds, incorporating diverse tactics into his play. His teammates began to notice, and soon, they too were eager to learn and integrate these newfound strategies. Lee's passion was igniting a flame, one that promised to light up the soccer world with a unique blend of Eastern determination and global finesse.

An Asian Star Shines Bright

Lee was quickly going from a local hero to a national figure of pride, thanks to his quick feet and smart mind. As he went from playing on crowded local fields to big national stadiums, his name started to sound like a promise of something special. People from all over his home country would gather around TVs to watch their homegrown ability shine against players with more experience. And he was amazed! With every game, Lee showed that he wasn't just another player. Instead, he was a great example of how much football in Asia still has to offer.

Lee was more than just a football player to the young players who wanted to be like him back home. He was a sign, a lighthouse pointing the way to worldwide fame. Children would try to copy his moves in alleys and fields, hoping that one day they, too, would be able to show off their roots on an international stage. Parents who usually didn't want their kids to go into sports started to change their minds when they saw Lee's potential for world success based on local values. Not only was it his own story, but it was also becoming an inspiring story for a whole generation.

Lee had a big effect on the rest of the world. The commentators, who had seen a lot of stars come and go, always spoke highly of "Lee from the East." They saw in him a unique mix of Eastern persistence and methods from around the world. People started talking about how Asian teams were getting better and better, and Lee was often at the center of these conversations. Every goal he scored and every game he won were not just personal successes. It was a loud and clear statement that Asian football had come to the world stage and was here to leave a lasting mark.

Lee's inspiring journey mirrors the unwavering determination and grit of Son Heung-min, who has become a beacon for Asian football on international grounds.

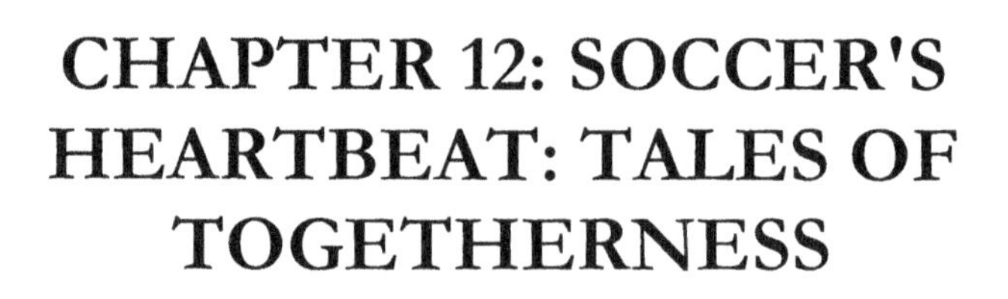

CHAPTER 12: SOCCER'S HEARTBEAT: TALES OF TOGETHERNESS

In the small town of Greenfield, where everyone knew each other and friends were more like extended family, there was a friendly rivalry that went back many years. On either side of town were two schools, Elmwood High and Pineview Prep, and their rivalry was famous. They fought over everything, from who could cheer the loudest at parades to who had the best science fair projects to who had the best Halloween outfits. But nothing, nothing at all, could compare to the excitement of their yearly soccer game.

It was like a town fair on the day of the game. The streets would be lined with flags, the kids would paint their faces with their school colors, and everyone in the town, young and old, would go to the soccer field to cheer for their favorite team. There would be a lot of chatter and energy in the air. One year, during a very tense game, when both teams were tied, the unthinkable happened: the ball burst. There were gasps all over the field. But Jamie from Elmwood and Rhea from Pineview, both of whom were determined, chose to sew the ball together with threads from their jerseys instead of letting it cause a fight.

Something changed in Greenfield because of this simple, heartwarming act. Even though the competition was still there, it became more friendly and fun. Yes, they still played and tried to score more than the other team, but now every game ended with smiles, laughter, and players from both teams getting together for a group photo. The fixed soccer ball was put in the town museum

as a simple but powerful symbol of togetherness and the magic of sportsmanship. It showed everyone that sometimes it's not about winning, but about playing together with heart.

The Unlikely Teammates

Even though Sunridge and Moonbrook are close by, the people there have lived apart for a long time. They didn't understand each other because they spoke different languages, had different holidays, and had different stories and songs. Children grew up hearing stories about the "other" town, which made the differences and mysteries seem even bigger.

One bright summer morning, a coach from a faraway city called Mr. Landon decided to start a small project. He had a dream of putting together a soccer team with people from both towns. People were not sure about the idea. Since the kids had always played against each other, the idea of being partners was strange to them. During the first few practices, people hesitated, didn't understand what was being said, and had a lot of confused looks on their faces. But as the days turned into weeks, a wonderful thing started to happen. After a goal, a nod, a motion, a clap, or a jump into the air became their common language. They found that words didn't always bring people together, but a common goal did.

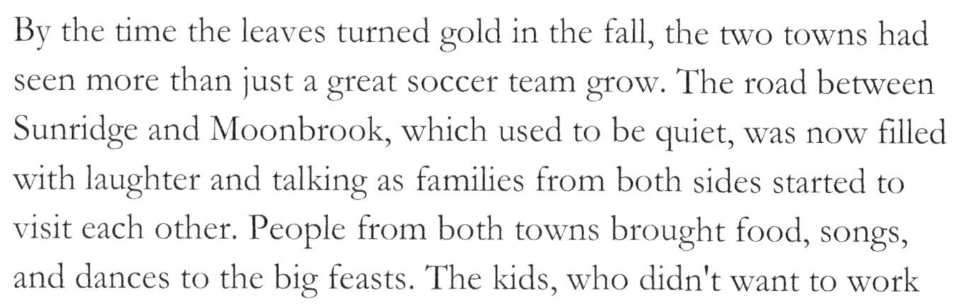

By the time the leaves turned gold in the fall, the two towns had seen more than just a great soccer team grow. The road between Sunridge and Moonbrook, which used to be quiet, was now filled with laughter and talking as families from both sides started to visit each other. People from both towns brought food, songs, and dances to the big feasts. The kids, who didn't want to work

together at first, became the link between two different worlds. Even though they were happy about their wins on the field, the real victory was the coming together of two towns thanks to the magic of soccer.

One Goal, Many Hearts

In the big world of international soccer, where the stakes were high and feelings often got out of hand, a match was set up between two countries that had been fighting for a long time. Fans and reporters got ready for what they thought would be a heated game on and off the field. This made the air tense. But when the referee blew the whistle, things changed in a way that no one expected.

From the first kick to the last whistle, both teams' players showed kindness and friendship that went beyond the game. It seemed like they all knew that they weren't just promoting their countries, but also the spirit of soccer. When a person fell, an opponent was always close by to help them up. During the breaks, people talked and laughed with each other, which made the fight less intense. When the game ended in a tie after a hard-fought battle, both teams agreed to take a picture together.

That one picture showed a moment of togetherness and unity that said a lot. It was a powerful lesson that soccer can bring people together, no matter how different they are. It was a celebration of what all soccer fans have in common: a love for the game and an understanding that, underneath the shirts and flags, they were all just players with the same interest. This touching picture became a symbol of how soccer can bring people together and remember the world that at its heart, soccer is about coming together and having fun playing together.

The heartwarming episodes in this chapter are inspired by countless acts of unity and togetherness in the world of soccer, where the sport mends divides, brings adversaries together, and stands as a symbol of unity and hope.

CONCLUSION: DREAM, BELIEVE, ACHIEVE

We have traveled through moving tales that have demonstrated the amazing power of the "beautiful game" in the enchanted world of soccer. It is more than just kicking a ball; it is a symbol of unity, hope, and limitless potential. Let's consider the important lessons these tales have to teach all young readers as we come to the end of our journey through them.

These tales mostly tell us that pursuing our aspirations is worthwhile. You can have huge ideas and work hard to make them come true, just like Tom, Sara, Moe, Christie, Nate, Suresh, Zara, and Lee did. One kick at a time, you can use the soccer pitch as a canvas to create your goals.

Every great accomplishment is fueled by belief. Tom was an inspiration because he thought that he could overcome his obstacles. Sara's confidence in her special abilities helped her to unanticipated stardom. Moe was raised in a small town but rose to the top of European football because he believed in the virtue of hard work. Christie had a strong confidence in the power of teamwork, which helped her team succeed. Nate was liked by everyone because he believed in the power of a smile.

Soccer teaches us the value of cooperation as well. We discover that when we come together and support one another, we can accomplish something remarkable. This lesson comes from Zara's squad in Afghanistan, where unity overcame hardship.

Finally, these tales serve as a reminder that soccer is more than simply a game; it is a universal language that unites people from all over the world. Soccer has the ability to motivate and bring people together whether it is played on a wintry field or in a busy city.

So, young readers, keep soccer's lessons in mind as you go on your own life journeys. Dream large, have confidence in yourself, collaborate with others, and speak with one voice. You are equipped with these teachings in your heart and are prepared to overcome any obstacle in your path and, like the protagonists of these tales, achieve greatness. The world is your playground; go forth and embellish it.

BONUS 1: POSITIVE AFFIRMATIONS FOR SUCCESS

I am unique and special in my own way.
I love and accept myself just as I am.
I believe in my abilities and talents.
I am capable of achieving great things.
I am full of endless possibilities.
I am confident in everything I do.
I am kind and compassionate towards others.
I choose to focus on the positive in every situation.
I am a source of positivity and light.
I am resilient and can overcome any challenge.
I am loved and cherished by my family and friends.
I have a bright and happy future ahead of me.
I am a good friend to others.
I am grateful for the little things in life.
I am a lifelong learner, and I love to learn new things.
I am in control of my thoughts and feelings.
I am always learning and growing.
I am surrounded by love and support.
I am open to new experiences and adventures.
I am a positive role model for others.
I am full of energy and enthusiasm.
I am capable of making a positive impact on the world.
I am responsible and make good choices.
I am confident in expressing my ideas and opinions.
I am a problem solver and can find solutions.
I am worthy of love and respect.
I am a good listener and a caring friend.
I am always improving and getting better.
I am patient and understanding.

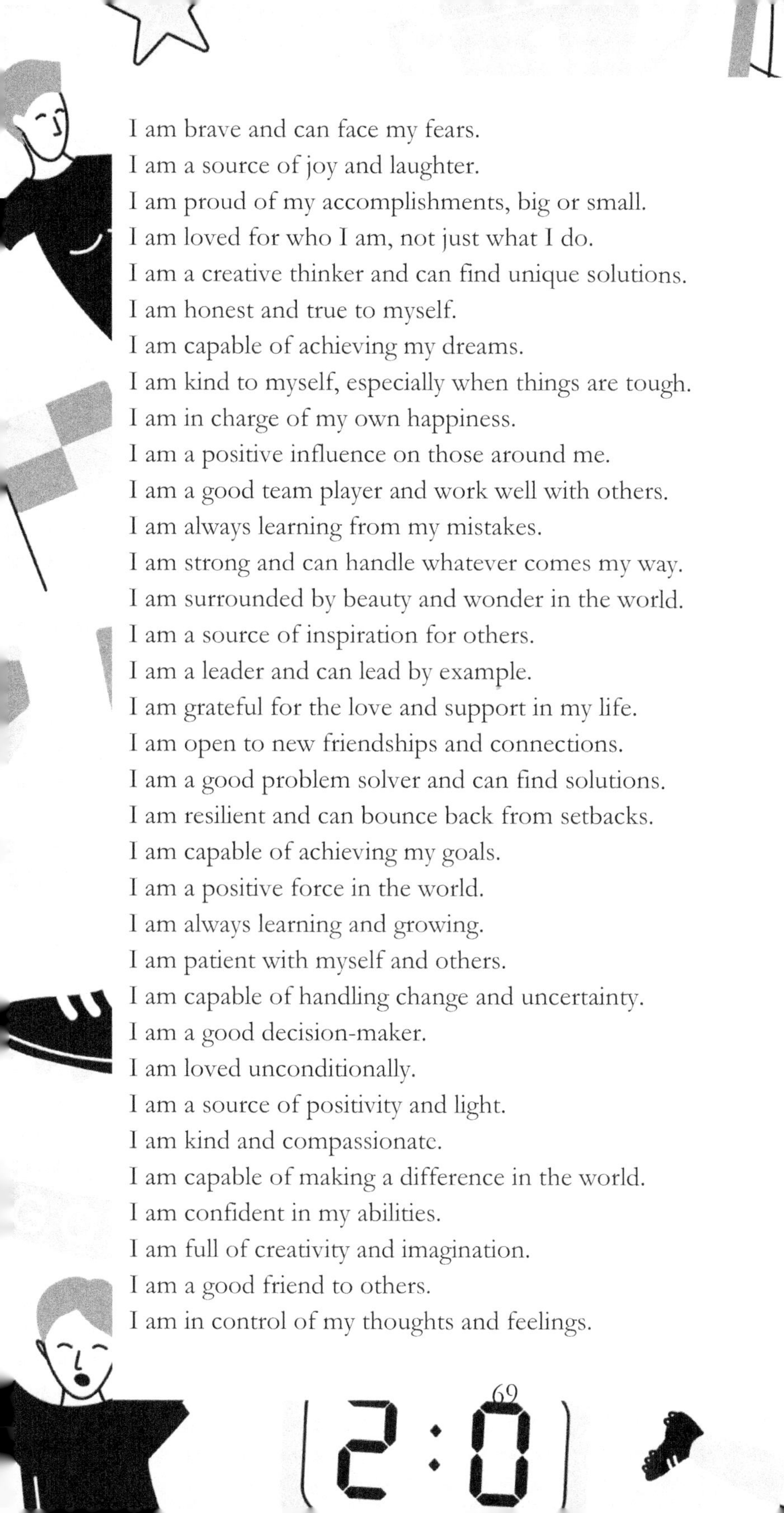

I am brave and can face my fears.
I am a source of joy and laughter.
I am proud of my accomplishments, big or small.
I am loved for who I am, not just what I do.
I am a creative thinker and can find unique solutions.
I am honest and true to myself.
I am capable of achieving my dreams.
I am kind to myself, especially when things are tough.
I am in charge of my own happiness.
I am a positive influence on those around me.
I am a good team player and work well with others.
I am always learning from my mistakes.
I am strong and can handle whatever comes my way.
I am surrounded by beauty and wonder in the world.
I am a source of inspiration for others.
I am a leader and can lead by example.
I am grateful for the love and support in my life.
I am open to new friendships and connections.
I am a good problem solver and can find solutions.
I am resilient and can bounce back from setbacks.
I am capable of achieving my goals.
I am a positive force in the world.
I am always learning and growing.
I am patient with myself and others.
I am capable of handling change and uncertainty.
I am a good decision-maker.
I am loved unconditionally.
I am a source of positivity and light.
I am kind and compassionate.
I am capable of making a difference in the world.
I am confident in my abilities.
I am full of creativity and imagination.
I am a good friend to others.
I am in control of my thoughts and feelings.

I am grateful for the love in my life.
I am a lifelong learner.
I am capable of achieving my dreams.
I am loved and cherished.
I am a source of joy and happiness.
I am responsible and make good choices.
I am confident in expressing myself.
I am always improving and growing.
I am patient and understanding.
I am brave and can face challenges head-on.
I am proud of my accomplishments.
I am capable of overcoming obstacles.
I am worthy of love and respect.
I am a good listener and friend.
I am always learning from my experiences.
I am strong and resilient.
I am surrounded by beauty and goodness.
I am a positive role model for others.
I am a leader and can inspire others.
I am open to new opportunities.
I am a problem solver and can find solutions.
I am honest and true to myself.
I am capable of achieving my goals.
I am kind to myself and others.
I am in charge of my own happiness.
I am a good team player and collaborator.
I am capable of handling challenges.
I am a source of inspiration for others.
I am always learning and growing.
I am patient and compassionate.
I am confident in my abilities.
I am a positive force in the world.
I am responsible and make good choices.
I am resilient and can bounce back from setbacks.

I am capable of achieving my dreams.
I am filled with love, happiness, and self-esteem.
I am a source of kindness and positivity.
I am a beacon of hope for those around me.
I am capable of handling whatever comes my way.
I am a loving and caring person.
I am always open to new possibilities.
I am filled with gratitude for the present moment.
I am a source of inspiration to others.
I am a responsible and dependable friend.
I am confident in my ability to learn and grow.
I am surrounded by opportunities for success.
I am a good problem solver and can find answers.
I am resilient and can adapt to change.
I am a positive influence on my peers.
I am a magnet for good things to come my way.
I am full of creativity and innovative ideas.
I am proud of the person I am becoming.
I am a loving and supportive family member.
I am always seeking ways to improve myself.
I am confident in expressing my true self.
I am capable of turning challenges into opportunities.
I am a source of joy and laughter for others.
I am grateful for the lessons I learn every day.
I am a compassionate and empathetic listener.
I am courageous and stand up for what is right.
I am a source of positivity in my community.
I am full of energy and enthusiasm for life.
I am capable of achieving my wildest dreams.
I am responsible for my own happiness.
I am a good communicator and can express myself well.
I am always open to learning from others.
I am strong and resilient, like a tree in a storm.
I am a friend who can be trusted and relied upon.

I am open to new experiences that expand my horizons.
I am a beacon of light even in the darkest moments.
I am surrounded by love and support every day.
I am a positive force for change in the world.
I am full of curiosity and a thirst for knowledge.
I am a good sport and can handle wins and losses gracefully.
I am confident in my ability to make a difference.
I am patient with myself and others.
I am capable of finding solutions to any problem.
I am worthy of all the good things that come my way.
I am a friend who brings joy to others.
I am in control of my own destiny.
I am open to new friendships and connections.
I am capable of achieving my highest goals.
I am a positive role model for those younger than me.
I am a loving and giving person.
I am always striving to be the best version of myself.
I am confident in my ability to handle adversity.
I am a source of happiness to my loved ones.
I am grateful for the simple pleasures in life.
I am a source of encouragement to others.
I am a responsible and reliable member of my family.
I am open to the wisdom of those who came before me.
I am strong and unshakable in my beliefs.
I am a good leader and inspire others to follow.
I am capable of achieving my dreams through hard work.
I am kind to myself, especially during difficult times.
I am a positive influence on my peers.
I am a magnet for success and happiness.
I am a creative problem solver.
I am proud of my accomplishments and achievements.
I am a source of comfort and support to others.
I am always open to new adventures.
I am surrounded by love and positive energy.

I am a force for good in the world.
I am curious and eager to explore new ideas.
I am a good sport and show sportsmanship in all I do.
I am confident in my ability to make a positive impact.
I am patient with myself as I grow and learn.
I am capable of finding solutions to challenges.
I am worthy of all the love and happiness in the world.
I am a friend who brings joy and laughter to others.
I am in charge of my own destiny and choices.
I am open to new friendships and connections.
I am capable of reaching my highest aspirations.
I am a positive example for my peers.
I am a source of love and kindness.
I am always striving to improve and learn.
I am confident in my ability to overcome obstacles.
I am a source of inspiration and motivation.
I am grateful for the love and support in my life.
I am responsible and make choices that align with my values.
I am resilient and can bounce back from challenges.
I am capable of achieving my dreams through hard work.
I am filled with love, kindness, and positivity.
I am open to new experiences that enrich my life.
I am a positive force for change in my community.
I am a continuous learner, always seeking knowledge.
I am confident in my abilities and talents.
I am a gracious winner and a good loser.
I am proud of my accomplishments, no matter how big or small.
I am a source of encouragement to my loved ones.
I am always open to new opportunities.
I am surrounded by love and positive energy every day.
I am a beacon of light even in challenging times.
I am confident in my ability to handle whatever comes my way.
I am a loving and caring friend to others.
I am full of gratitude for the present moment.

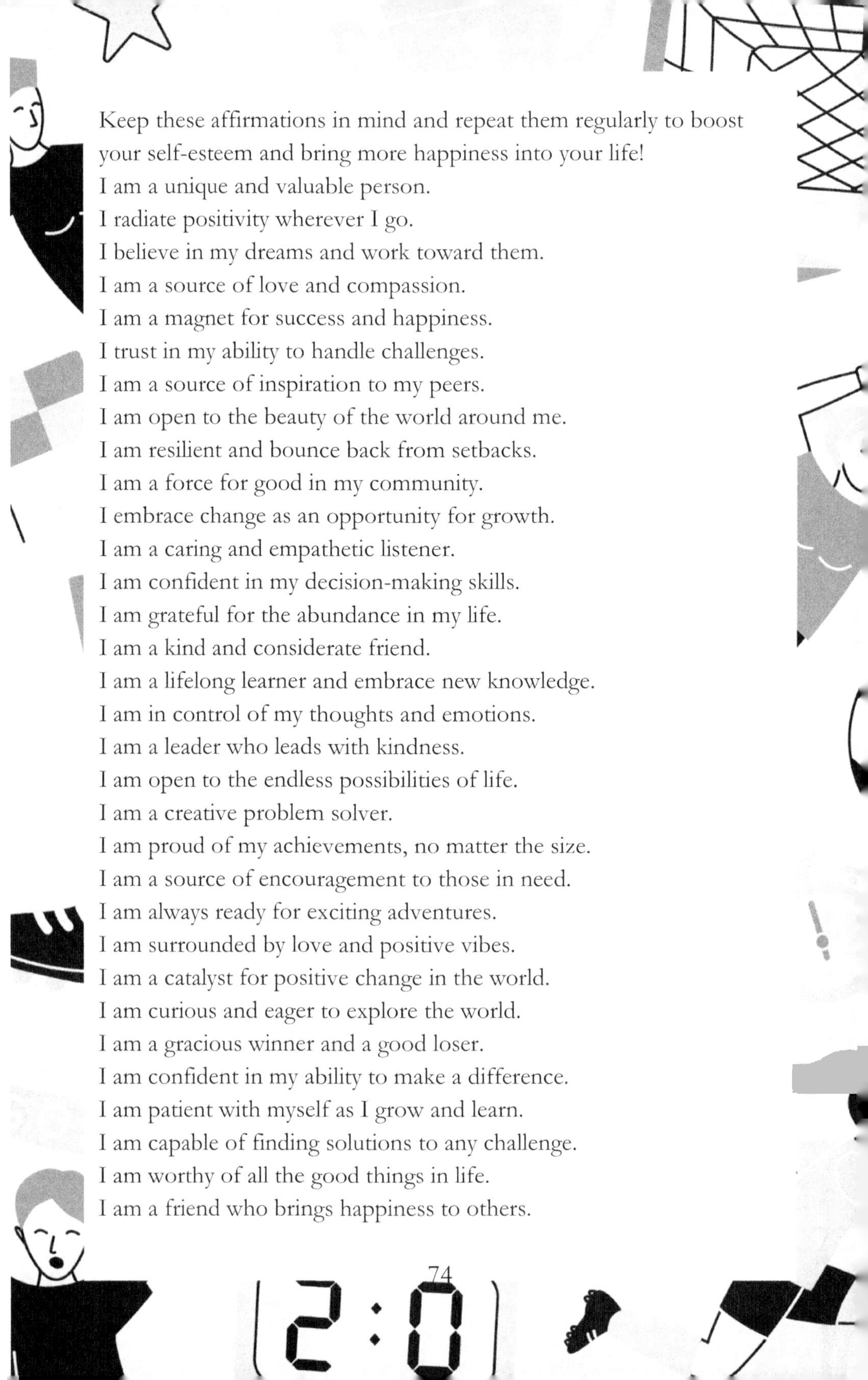

Keep these affirmations in mind and repeat them regularly to boost your self-esteem and bring more happiness into your life!

I am a unique and valuable person.
I radiate positivity wherever I go.
I believe in my dreams and work toward them.
I am a source of love and compassion.
I am a magnet for success and happiness.
I trust in my ability to handle challenges.
I am a source of inspiration to my peers.
I am open to the beauty of the world around me.
I am resilient and bounce back from setbacks.
I am a force for good in my community.
I embrace change as an opportunity for growth.
I am a caring and empathetic listener.
I am confident in my decision-making skills.
I am grateful for the abundance in my life.
I am a kind and considerate friend.
I am a lifelong learner and embrace new knowledge.
I am in control of my thoughts and emotions.
I am a leader who leads with kindness.
I am open to the endless possibilities of life.
I am a creative problem solver.
I am proud of my achievements, no matter the size.
I am a source of encouragement to those in need.
I am always ready for exciting adventures.
I am surrounded by love and positive vibes.
I am a catalyst for positive change in the world.
I am curious and eager to explore the world.
I am a gracious winner and a good loser.
I am confident in my ability to make a difference.
I am patient with myself as I grow and learn.
I am capable of finding solutions to any challenge.
I am worthy of all the good things in life.
I am a friend who brings happiness to others.

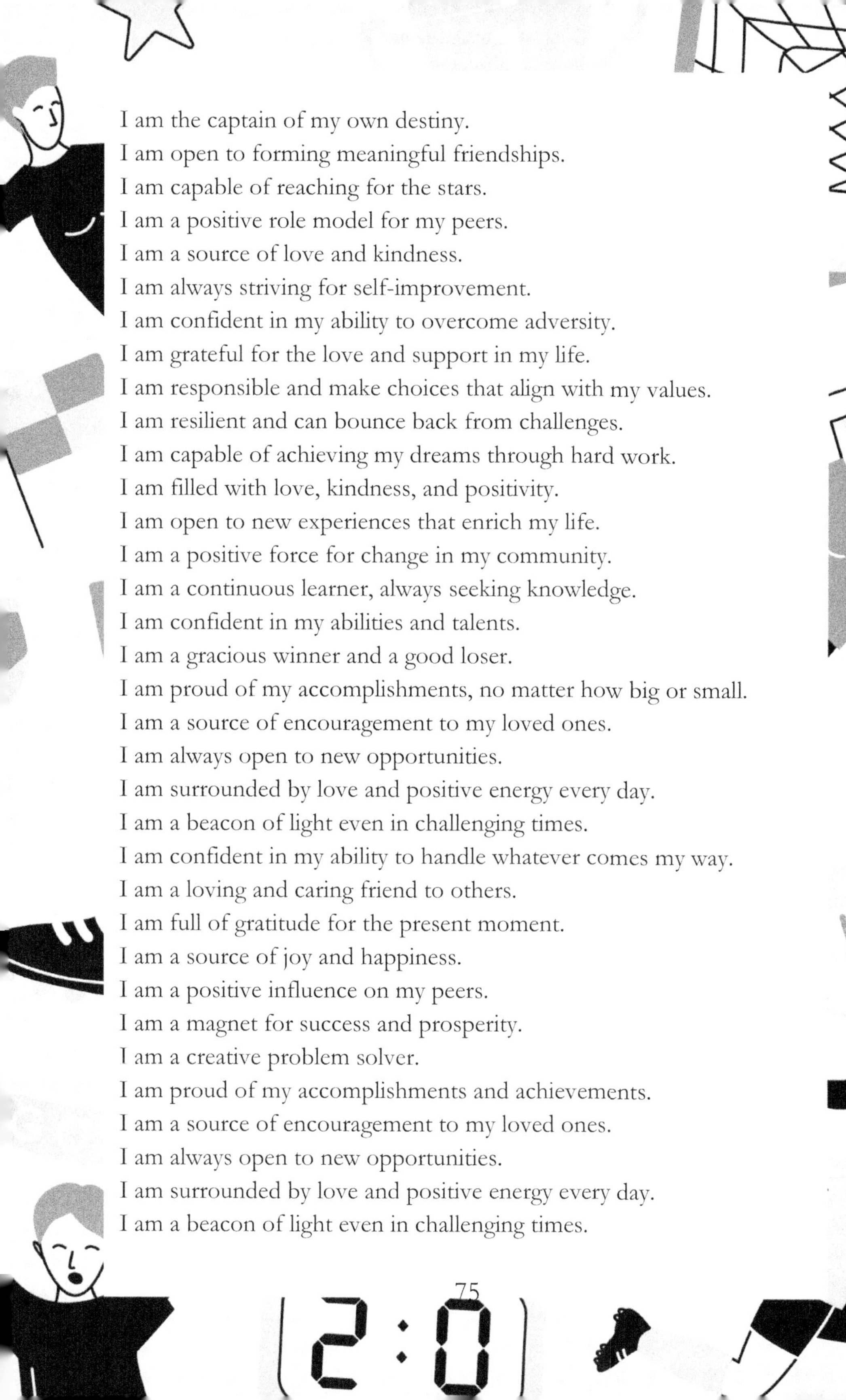

I am the captain of my own destiny.
I am open to forming meaningful friendships.
I am capable of reaching for the stars.
I am a positive role model for my peers.
I am a source of love and kindness.
I am always striving for self-improvement.
I am confident in my ability to overcome adversity.
I am grateful for the love and support in my life.
I am responsible and make choices that align with my values.
I am resilient and can bounce back from challenges.
I am capable of achieving my dreams through hard work.
I am filled with love, kindness, and positivity.
I am open to new experiences that enrich my life.
I am a positive force for change in my community.
I am a continuous learner, always seeking knowledge.
I am confident in my abilities and talents.
I am a gracious winner and a good loser.
I am proud of my accomplishments, no matter how big or small.
I am a source of encouragement to my loved ones.
I am always open to new opportunities.
I am surrounded by love and positive energy every day.
I am a beacon of light even in challenging times.
I am confident in my ability to handle whatever comes my way.
I am a loving and caring friend to others.
I am full of gratitude for the present moment.
I am a source of joy and happiness.
I am a positive influence on my peers.
I am a magnet for success and prosperity.
I am a creative problem solver.
I am proud of my accomplishments and achievements.
I am a source of encouragement to my loved ones.
I am always open to new opportunities.
I am surrounded by love and positive energy every day.
I am a beacon of light even in challenging times.

I am confident in my ability to handle whatever comes my way.
I am a loving and caring friend to others.
I am full of gratitude for the present moment.
I am a source of joy and happiness.
I am a positive influence on my peers.
I am a magnet for success and prosperity.
I am confident in my ability to achieve my goals.
I am open to receiving love and support from others.
I am responsible for my own happiness.
I am a source of motivation to those around me.
I am resilient and can overcome any obstacle.
I am capable of accomplishing great things.
I am a beacon of positivity in the world.
I am a source of comfort to my loved ones.
I am always open to new experiences.
I am surrounded by abundance and prosperity.
I am a catalyst for positive change in my community.
I am a constant learner and love acquiring knowledge.
I am confident in my unique talents and gifts.
I am open to new challenges that help me grow.
I am a source of encouragement to those in need.
I am capable of making a lasting impact on the world.
I am full of optimism and hope for the future.
I am a positive force in the lives of others.
I am grateful for the lessons I learn from every experience.
I am a reliable and trustworthy friend.
I am open to the wisdom of those who came before me.
I am strong and unwavering in my beliefs.
I am a leader who guides with compassion.
I am capable of turning my dreams into reality.
I am kind to myself, especially in challenging moments.
I am a beacon of inspiration to those around me.
I am filled with self-love, happiness, and confidence.

2 : 0

BONUS 2: SOCCER QUIZ

PART 1

Which soccer legend is nicknamed "The Black Pearl"?
a) Cristiano Ronaldo
b) Pelé
c) Thierry Henry
d) Ronaldinho

Which team did the legendary Paolo Maldini spend most of his career with?
a) AC Milan
b) FC Barcelona
c) Real Madrid
d) Juventus

Which Brazilian soccer player is famous for his style of play known as "samba football"?
a) Ronaldinho
b) Romário
c) Kaka
d) Rivaldo

Who was the first player to score 1000 goals in official matches?
a) Cristiano Ronaldo
b) Pelé
c) Ferenc Puskás
d) Josef Bican

Which former English soccer player scored the famous "Hand of God" goal during a 1986 World Cup match?
a) David Beckham
b) Wayne Rooney
c) Gary Lineker
d) Diego Maradona

Who is the coach known for his long and successful career with Manchester United?
a) Pep Guardiola
b) José Mourinho
c) Sir Alex Ferguson
d) Arsène Wenger

Which national soccer team has won the most FIFA World Cups?
a) Brazil
b) Germany
c) Italy
d) Argentina

Which Argentine forward is known for being Lionel Messi's teammate at both FC Barcelona and Paris Saint-Germain?
a) Gonzalo Higuaín
b) Sergio Agüero
c) Ángel Di María
d) Ezequiel Lavezzi

Who was the first player to be awarded the Ballon d'Or?
a) Johan Cruyff
b) Alfredo Di Stéfano
c) Pelé
d) Stanley Matthews

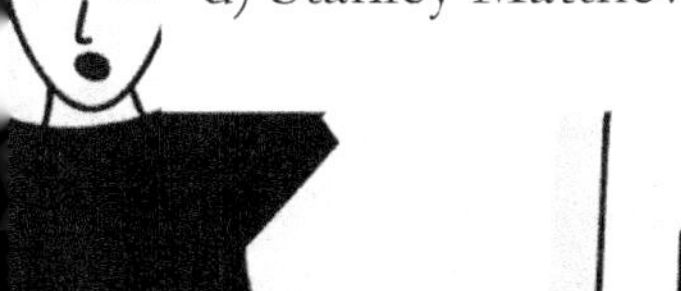

Answers:

b) Pelé
a) AC Milan
a) Ronaldinho
d) Josef Bican
d) Diego Maradona
c) Sir Alex Ferguson
a) Brazil
b) Sergio Agüero
d) Stanley Matthews
I hope this quiz adds an interactive and educational element to your book "Inspirational Soccer Stories for Young Readers." Enjoy!

PART 2

Which legendary goalkeeper is often referred to as the "Black Spider"?
a) Lev Yashin
b) Gianluigi Buffon
c) Iker Casillas
d) Dino Zoff

Who is known as the "Egyptian King" and plays for Liverpool FC?
a) Mo Salah (Mohamed Salah)
b) Sadio Mané
c) Roberto Firmino
d) Virgil van Dijk

Which country did the iconic Dutch soccer player Johan Cruyff represent in international matches?
a) Netherlands
b) Germany
c) Spain
d) France

What was the nickname of the famous Brazilian striker Ronaldo Luís Nazário de Lima?
a) R9
b) CR7
c) Neymar Jr.
d) Ronaldinho

Which Italian defender is widely regarded as one of the greatest defenders in soccer history and is known as "Il Capitano"?

a) Alessandro Nesta
b) Fabio Cannavaro
c) Franco Baresi
d) Paolo Maldini

Which soccer legend was a crucial part of the "Class of '92" at Manchester United?
a) Ryan Giggs
b) Paul Scholes
c) Roy Keane
d) Peter Schmeichel

Who is the all-time top scorer for the German national team and played for Bayern Munich for most of his club career?
a) Miroslav Klose
b) Thomas Müller
c) Oliver Kahn
d) Philipp Lahm

Which Portuguese soccer legend won the UEFA European Championship (Euro) with his national team in 2016?
a) Luís Figo
b) Deco
c) Eusébio
d) Cristiano Ronaldo

Which Argentine forward is famous for his incredible dribbling skills and is often compared to Diego Maradona?
a) Gonzalo Higuaín
b) Carlos Tevez
c) Juan Román Riquelme
d) Lionel Messi

Who is the current head coach of the England national soccer team as of 2023?
a) Gareth Southgate
b) Roy Hodgson
c) Sam Allardyce
d) Harry Redknapp

Answers:

a) Lev Yashin
a) Mo Salah (Mohamed Salah)
a) Netherlands
a) R9
d) Paolo Maldini
a) Ryan Giggs
a) Miroslav Klose
d) Cristiano Ronaldo
d) Lionel Messi
a) Gareth Southgate
Feel free to use these additional questions to enhance the quiz in your book. Enjoy!

PART 3

Who is the iconic French soccer player known for his elegance on the field and his success with Arsenal FC?
a) Zinedine Zidane
b) Thierry Henry
c) Patrick Vieira
d) Marcel Desailly

Which Brazilian midfielder is often referred to as "The Maestro" for his exceptional playmaking skills?
a) Kaká
b) Ronaldinho
c) Rivaldo
d) Zico

Which legendary English striker was the all-time top scorer for both Manchester United and the England national team?
a) Alan Shearer
b) Gary Lineker
c) Wayne Rooney
d) Michael Owen

Who is the Italian goalkeeper famous for his incredible reflexes and long tenure at Juventus FC?
a) Gianluigi Buffon
b) Dino Zoff
c) Angelo Peruzzi
d) Francesco Toldo

Which Dutch soccer legend was known for his total football philosophy and his time as both a player and coach at Ajax and Barcelona?
a) Frank Rijkaard
b) Ruud Gullit
c) Dennis Bergkamp
d) Johan Cruyff

Who is the Brazilian forward famous for his blistering speed and is often called "The Arrow"?
a) Ronaldo
b) Romário
c) Neymar Jr.
d) Robinho

Which Argentine goalkeeper is considered one of the greatest shot-stoppers of all time and had a legendary career at River Plate?
a) Sergio Romero
b) Ubaldo Fillol
c) Emiliano Martínez
d) Juan Pablo Carrizo

Which Spanish midfielder, known for his exceptional passing and vision, played a key role in Barcelona's tiki-taka style of play?
a) Andrés Iniesta
b) Xavi Hernandez
c) Cesc Fàbregas
d) Sergio Busquets

Who is the Brazilian defender who won three FIFA World Cups (1958, 1962, 1970) and is considered one of the greatest soccer players of all time?
a) Pelé
b) Romário
c) Cafu
d) Roberto Carlos

Which legendary German striker was known for his goal-scoring prowess and won the FIFA World Cup in 1974 as both a player and coach?
a) Franz Beckenbauer
b) Gerd Müller
c) Karl-Heinz Rummenigge
d) Miroslav Klose

Answers:

b) Thierry Henry
d) Zico
a) Alan Shearer
a) Gianluigi Buffon
d) Johan Cruyff
d) Robinho
b) Ubaldo Fillol
b) Xavi Hernandez
d) Roberto Carlos
a) Franz Beckenbauer
Enjoy these additional questions for your quiz!
PART 4

Which Portuguese soccer legend was known as "The Black Panther" and had a successful career with Benfica?
a) Cristiano Ronaldo
b) Eusébio
c) Luís Figo
d) Rui Costa

Who is the Brazilian striker known for his acrobatic goals and bicycle kicks, earning him the nickname "The Bicycle Kick King"?
a) Adriano
b) Bebeto
c) Zlatan Ibrahimović
d) Ronaldinho

Which English midfielder is famous for his long-range goals and was known as "Golden Balls" during his career?
a) Frank Lampard
b) David Beckham
c) Steven Gerrard
d) Paul Scholes

Which Italian striker, known for his clinical finishing, was part of Italy's 2006 FIFA World Cup-winning team?
a) Alessandro Del Piero
b) Luca Toni
c) Filippo Inzaghi
d) Francesco Totti

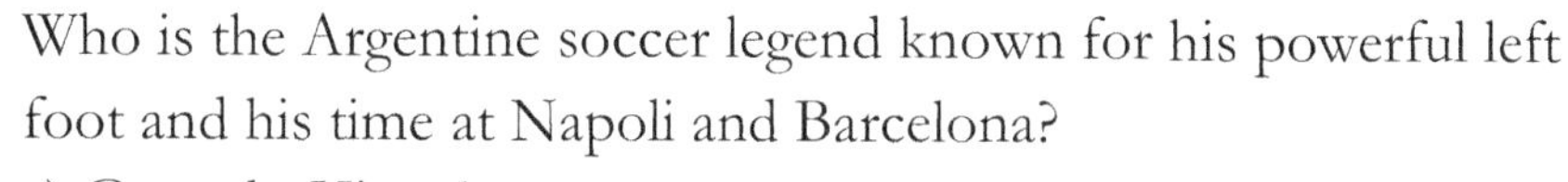

Who is the Argentine soccer legend known for his powerful left foot and his time at Napoli and Barcelona?
a) Gonzalo Higuaín
b) Carlos Tevez

c) Juan Román Riquelme
d) Diego Maradona

Which Spanish goalkeeper, considered one of the best in the world, spent the majority of his career at Real Madrid?
a) Iker Casillas
b) Xabi Alonso
c) Carles Puyol
d) Fernando Torres

Who is the French midfielder known for his elegance on the ball and his time at Juventus and Real Madrid?
a) Zinedine Zidane
b) Michel Platini
c) Alain Giresse
d) Didier Deschamps

Which Brazilian soccer legend is often referred to as "The Phenomenon" and had a successful career with Barcelona and Inter Milan?
a) Romário
b) Rivaldo
c) Ronaldo
d) Ronaldinho

Who is the Dutch forward famous for his speed, dribbling, and long-range shots, known as "The Flying Dutchman"?
a) Ruud Gullit
b) Dennis Bergkamp
c) Robin van Persie
d) Arjen Robben

Which German midfielder is known for his incredible vision and passing ability, earning him the nickname "The Little Mozart"?
a) Bastian Schweinsteiger
b) Mesut Özil
c) Michael Ballack
d) Thomas Müller

Answers:

b) Eusébio
d) Ronaldinho
b) David Beckham
b) Luca Toni
d) Diego Maradona
a) Iker Casillas
a) Zinedine Zidane
c) Ronaldo
d) Arjen Robben
b) Mesut Özil

Do Not Go Yet; One Last Thing To Do

If you enjoyed this book or found it useful, I'd be very grateful if you'd post a short review on Amazon. Your support does make a difference, and I read all the reviews personally so I can get your feedback and make this book even better.

Thanks again for your support!